HENRY HUDSON

HENRY HUDSON

Great Explorers of the World

Discoverer of the Hudson River

Jeff C. Young

Enslow Publishers, Inc.
40 Industrial Road
Box 398
Berkeley Heights, NJ 07922
USA
http://www.enslow.com

Library of Congress Cataloging-in-Publication Data

Young, Jeff C., 1948-
 Henry Hudson : discoverer of the Hudson River / Jeff C. Young.
    p. cm. — (Great Explorers of the world)
 Includes bibliographical references and index.
 Summary: "Examines the life of explorer Henry Hudson, including his
quest for the elusive Northeast passage, his discovery of the Hudson
River, and his mysterious death"—Provided by publisher.
 ISBN-13: 978-1-59845-123-8 (alk. paper)
 ISBN-10: 1-59845-123-5 (alk. paper)
 1. Hudson, Henry, d. 1611—Juvenile literature. 2. Explorers—America—
Biography—Juvenile literature. 3. Explorers—Great Britain—
Biography—Juvenile literature. 4. America—Discovery and exploration—
Juvenile literature. I. Title.
 E129.H8Y68 2009
 910.92—dc22
 [B]
                                   2008030752

Printed in the United States of America

10 9 8 7 6 5 4 3 2 1

To Our Readers: We have done our best to make sure all Internet Addresses in this book were active
and appropriate when we went to press. However, the author and the publisher have no control over
and assume no liability for the material available on those Internet sites or on other Web sites they may
link to. Any comments or suggestions can be sent by e-mail to comments@enslow.com or to the address
on the back cover.

♻ Enslow Publishers, Inc., is committed to printing our books on recycled paper. The paper in every
book contains 10% to 30% post-consumer waste (PCW). The cover board on the outside of each book
contains 100% PCW. Our goal is to do our part to help young people and the environment too!

Illustration Credits: Courtesy of the Art Commission of the City of New York, p. 11; Enslow
Publishers, Inc., pp. 30, 67, 91; The Granger Collection, New York, pp. 3, 20, 25, 54–55, 72–73, 76,
78–79, 96; © Jupiterimages Corporation, pp. 14–15; Lee Gillen, p. 102; Library of Congress, pp. 26, 68;
Courtesy Markstemp58@flickr, pp. 60–61; NOAA, p. 47; © North Wind Picture Archives, pp. 44–45;
Public Domain Image, p. 81; Richard Huber, *Treasury of Fantastic and Mythological Creatures* (Toronto:
Dover Publications, Inc., 1981), p. 42; © Shutterstock®, pp. 32–33, 34.

Ship Illustration Used in Chapter Openers: Library of Congress.

Cover Illustration: The Granger Collection, New York (Portrait of Henry Hudson).

Contents

EXPLORER TIMELINE

1607—The Muscovy Company in London hires Henry Hudson to find a Northeast Passage to China.

—*May 1*, Hudson leaves England on his first voyage aboard the *Hopewell*.

—*September 15*, Hudson and his crew return to London after failing to find the Northeast Passage.

1608—*April 22*, Hudson departs on his second voyage aboard the *Hopewell* to begin another search for a Northeast Passage.

—*August 7*, An entry in the *Hopewell*'s log indicates that Hudson may have had to quell a mutiny.

—*August 26*, Hudson and his crew return from their second voyage after failing to find a Northeast Passage.

—*September–October*, After failing to raise money for a third voyage, Hudson travels to Holland and meets with the directors of the Dutch East India Company.

1609—*January 8*, Hudson is hired by the Dutch East India Company to look for a Northeast Passage.

—*April 4 or 6*, Hudson leaves Amsterdam harbor commanding the *Half Moon*.

—*May 19*, Hudson survives a possible mutiny and changes course by sailing southwest.

—*July 2*, Hudson and his crew reach the coast of Newfoundland.

- *July 18*, The *Half Moon* lands at Penobscot Bay.

- *September 12*, Hudson discovers the mouth of the Hudson River in New York.

- *September*, The *Half Moon* sails up the Hudson River in search of a Northwest Passage to the Orient.

- *October 4*, Hudson begins a return journey to England after failing to find a Northwest Passage.

- *November 7*, Hudson and his crew arrive in England. The English government forbids them from traveling to Holland or working for a foreign government again.

1610—*April 7*, After getting some wealthy merchants to sponsor him for a search for a Northwest Passage, Hudson sails out of England on his ship, the *Discovery*.

- *November 1*, After vainly searching for the passage, Hudson and his crew spend a miserable winter on the shore of James Bay.

1611— *June 22*, A mutiny led by crewmen Robert Juet, William Wilson, and Henry Greene takes Hudson by surprise. Hudson, his son, and seven crewmembers still loyal to him are cast adrift in a shallop. Presumably, they all perish since none of them are ever seen again.

- *July 28*, Four mutineers are slain by Inuit.

- *October*, The *Discovery* returns to England with the remaining mutineers aboard.

1618— *July 24*, Three of the surviving mutineers are tried for their part in the uprising, but none of them are convicted.

Chapter 1

Mutiny!

For seven miserable months, the crew of Henry Hudson's ship, the *Discovery*, had been marooned in the frozen waters of Hudson Bay. During that time, the unrelenting and numbing cold weather had intensified the crew's gnawing hunger pangs and undermined their faith in Hudson. They were homesick, hungry, and rebellious.

Hudson was on his fourth and final voyage attempting to find a northern sea route from Europe to the Orient, today called Asia. The commonly used southern routes, which went around Africa, were controlled by Spain and Portugal. Hudson had first sailed for England, then for Holland, to find a yet undiscovered northern route. Those two countries wanted to get a share of the lucrative trade with Asia.

On or around November 10, 1610, Hudson's ship, the *Discovery*, became stuck in the frozen waters of subarctic North America. Hudson believed that building a house onshore would give his crew a safe refuge until the arrival of warmer spring weather melted the gripping ice.

Hudson ordered the ship's carpenter, Philip Staffe, to build a house. Staffe had been unfailingly loyal to his captain. He was a veteran of previous voyages with Hudson. But for the first time, Staffe did not obey an order from his captain.

Staffe knew that building a house in the midst of winter was a nearly impossible task. The wood planks would freeze to the ground. Cold fingers would barely be able to grip a hammer and pound nails in the bone-chilling winter. He sent word to his captain that "he neither would nor could goe in hand with such work."[1]

Staffe's refusal infuriated Hudson. He threatened the defiant carpenter with a hanging. A few minutes later, Hudson regained his composure, but the damage was done. Several crew members had seen their enraged captain make a death threat. Hudson would never regain their loyalty.

Staffe built the house, but another incident further alienated Hudson's demoralized crew. In mid-November, John Williams, the ship's gunner, died. At that time, it was customary to auction off the belongings of a crew member who died at sea. The proceeds would go to the deceased sailor's next of kin when the ship returned home.

Prior to the auction, a crew member named Henry Greene asked Hudson to give him a gray cloth coat that had belonged to Williams. Hudson

Henry Hudson

ignored the established custom and etiquette by giving the coat to Greene.

Apparently, Hudson changed his mind after Greene had gone hunting onshore with Staffe. Since Hudson had quarreled with Staffe, he felt that Greene was being disloyal to him. Hudson took the coat from Greene and gave it to another crew member.

When Greene protested his actions, Hudson threatened to withhold his wages. A once loyal crew member was now an avowed enemy of Hudson.

As the winter worsened, the food supply steadily dwindled. The game the crew had been hunting was disappearing. When there were cracks in the ice for casting nets, only a few fish could be dredged up. Crew members were sent ashore to forage for anything edible. They went into the woods, down into the valleys, and up over the hills searching for "all things that had any show of substance in them, how vile soever."[2]

The hunting party found only a few frogs. They dug up roots and even began eating the moss off the frozen ground. Abacuk Prickett, who kept a journal of the ill-fated voyage, noted how distasteful their diet was: "Nothing was spared, including moss of the ground, compared to which rotten wood is better, and the frog, which in breeding time is as loathsome as the toad."[3]

The lack of food and poor diet were affecting more than the crew's sagging morale. They were adversely affecting their health. The sickly crew contracted scurvy, a disease caused by a shortage of vitamin C in the diet. They suffered greatly from the disease's symptoms: bleeding gums, swollen limbs, and wounds that would not heal. Rumors began spreading that Hudson was secretly hoarding food and sharing it with favored members of the crew.

As spring approached, the crew's spirits were momentarily lifted by the unexpected visit of an Inuit. Hudson and the crew hoped that the visitor would be a possible source of food. Hudson asked his crew to donate their knives and hatchets to trade with the Inuit for food. They gave the Inuit a few trinkets—a mirror, a few colorful buttons, and a hatchet.

The Inuit promised to return the next day with items to trade. The following day, he returned with a sled loaded with two beaver skins and two deer skins. He had not understood that the men were seeking food, not skins.

Around mid-June, ice melted, freeing the *Discovery*. Hudson continued to alienate his crew by continuing his explorations instead of returning to England. Some of the crew, led by Greene, planned to desert the ship. But on the day that they planned to escape, Hudson thwarted their

In winter, James Bay is choked with ice. It was through these waters that Henry Hudson navigated the *Discovery* on his fourth voyage.

scheme. He took the rowboat that the deserters had planned to steal.

Hudson announced to his crew that he was taking the boat to look for Inuit on shore who could help them with food and other necessities. When he returned empty-handed, the crew's morale sank even lower. Hudson wisely decided that the *Discovery* would return to England, and he ordered the crew to prepare the ship for its return voyage.

Before sailing for home, Hudson had all the bread removed from the storage room. He ordered it to be evenly distributed among the crew. Each sailor received a pound of bread. From Friday morning to Sunday noon, they cast their nets for fish to supplement their bread ration. The catch was meager. The hungry crew hauled in about eighty small fish. In his journal, Prickett called the small catch "a poor relief for so many hungry bellies."[4]

Once the *Discovery* left the bay, Hudson had another food rationing. This time, he handed out the cheese that was left. Every crew member received three-and-a-half pounds, but there were complaints. Some crew members felt they should receive a daily ration. That would have kept the famished sailors from eating all of their allotment at once.

Hudson defended his decision by saying that some of the cheese had already spoiled. By handing it all out at once, each sailor had an equal amount of good and bad cheese. Still, some men quickly ate their entire ration. Then rumors resurfaced that Hudson was holding back on food. Some men claimed that there were nine cheeses on board and Hudson had only distributed five.

The food distribution created further problems because some crew members did not have the willpower to keep from gorging themselves. Greene ate a week's worth of bread in just three days. Another crew member, William Wilson, became ill from his binge eating. Wilson ate a two-week ration of bread in one day.

Since the problems with a lack of food persisted, Hudson made a drastic decision. He ordered crew member Nicholas Simmes to open each sailor's sea chest and search for stolen or hoarded food. That would be the last order that Hudson would give. Simmes reportedly found thirty loaves of bread. Yet the offenders went unpunished, and rumors continued that Hudson was hiding a personal supply of bread, cheese, and liquor in the captain's quarters.

On or about June 21, 1611, Greene and Wilson confided to Prickett that a mutiny was imminent. Their plan was to capture Hudson and place him in a shallop with the sickest and weakest members

of the crew. Once the shallop was loaded, it would be cast adrift.

In his journal, Prickett wrote, "When I heard this, I marvelled to hear so much from them, considering that they were married men, and had wives and children, and that for their sakes they should not commit so foul a thing."[5] Prickett claims that he warned them that they would be facing a hanging when they returned to England.

Greene replied that "he would rather be hanged at home than starved abroad."[6]

Wilson and Greene still tried to persuade Prickett to join in the mutiny. When Prickett refused, Greene threatened to place Prickett in the shallop with Hudson and the other sickly sailors. Prickett probably realized that a mutiny was inevitable. He told Greene that if there were no other remedy, then "the will of God be done."[7] Prickett did win one concession—he convinced Greene and Wilson to postpone their plan for mutiny until the following morning.

As the sun rose, the mutineers began putting their plan into action. The sound of the cook pouring water into a kettle was the signal to start. A carpenter, John King, was the first to be seized. He was quickly and quietly subdued before being placed in the ship's hold.

Hudson was captured a few minutes later. Matthews and crewman John Thomas grabbed the doomed captain when he walked on the ship's deck. They pinned Hudson's arms behind him while Wilson tied up his arms. In a matter of seconds, Hudson was completely helpless.

The few sailors who were still loyal to Hudson were unarmed or lying sick in their bunks. It took the mutineers only a few minutes to establish complete control of the ship. Hudson, his son John, and seven crew members were herded into the shallop. The deposed captain and crew members were allowed to take one gun with powder and shot, a little bit of grain, an iron pot, and a few spears.

While the shallop was being lowered into the water, the mutineers began ransacking the ship. They found some extra food provisions in Hudson's cabin, but they were no more that any prudent captain would have held back for an emergency. There was no cache of liquor, but the mutineers did find one large cask of beer.

After sailing clear of the ice, the mutineers severed the towrope tethering the shallop. The sickly and dispirited sailors aboard the shallop watched the *Discovery* slowly fade from view. To distance themselves from the sight of the shallop, the mutineers unfurled all the sails. Prickett noted that the *Discovery* "flew away as though from an enemy."[8]

The *Discovery* crew mutinied against Henry Hudson in June 1611.

To this day, the fate of Henry Hudson and his crew of castaways remains unknown. Among the native Cree, there are stories that the sailors survived after settling on the shores of James Bay on the western coast of Quebec, Canada. But there is no evidence to support those tales. The most likely occurrence is that they slowly starved to death while vainly hoping to be rescued.

Henry Hudson never found the fabled northern passage to Asia. Although he failed in his mission, Hudson is not considered a failure. His voyages made it possible for future explorers to avoid the uncharted waters that trapped him.

Chapter 2

The Quest for Asia

The birth and early years of Henry Hudson are as mysterious as his death. Prior to Hudson's first voyage in 1607, there are no records of the famous explorer and navigator.

Usually documents such as diaries, deeds, church records, and the written remembrances of friends and family can be used to document a person's life. In Hudson's case, none of those items exists or has been found. There are some probable, if not provable, facts about Hudson.

Historians believe that he was a descendant of another Henry Hudson who served in the London city government as an alderman. They also think that Hudson may have been related to some officers in the Muscovy Company, which later employed him to search for a Northeast Passage to China.

It is known that Hudson was married, and his wife was named Katherine. It is also a reported fact that they lived in a house near the Tower of London. Birth records indicate that they had three sons: Oliver, John, and Richard. Obviously, Hudson had several years of experience as a sailor and possibly as a navigator before making his first voyage. Yet there are no documents to show how he acquired that experience.

There is not even an accurate portrait or likeness of Hudson. Historians have not been able to find any portrait or drawing of Hudson that was made during his lifetime. The most widely published portrait of Hudson depicts him as a dapper-looking man with large eyes, a prominent sloping nose, and a neatly trimmed moustache and goatee. There are no written descriptions of his physical appearance. The few certain facts about him come from ship's logs, journals, and letters relating to Hudson's four voyages.

FARAWAY LANDS

In the sixteenth and seventeenth centuries, several European nations were competing to discover new lands and establish trade relations with faraway countries. Doing that would expand each nation's wealth and influence. England, Holland, France, Spain, Russia, and Portugal all financed explorers to find new lands and new, shorter routes to lands that they were trading with.

All of these countries were greatly interested in finding new sea routes to China and India, rich lands in Asia, then known as the Orient or the Far East. These lands were rich in highly desired

This is the most widely published portrait of Hudson. Historians have not found any portrait of Hudson made during his lifetime.

goods like silks, gold, tea, porcelain, jade, and spices, such as pepper.

The most common routes went south around the African continent. Spain and Portugal controlled those routes, so other countries searched for a northern passage to Asia.

By the early 1600s, the Muscovy Company was vying to find the undiscovered northern passage to Asia. A shorter, quicker route meant reduced travel times and increased profits for the traders

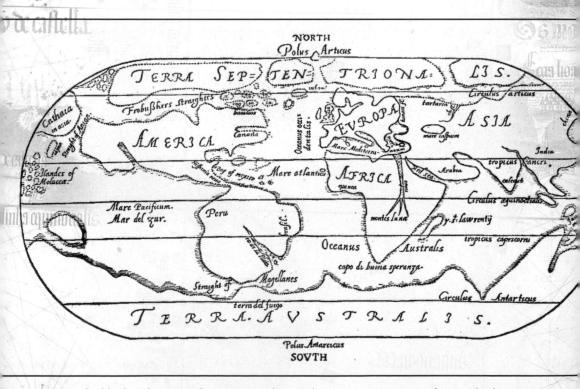

In Hudson's time, there was only one known sea route to Asia, which went around Africa. However, Spain and Portugal controlled this route. The only other way to get goods from Asia was to travel over land on a route called the Silk Road. This made finding another passage to Asia so valuable. Martin Forbisher depicted the Northwest Passage in his 1578 map.

and merchants. At that time, several of the world's leading geographers believed that it was possible to sail across the North Pole to reach the Orient.

Although no one had explored the North Pole at that time, it was known that the sun did not set in that area during the summer months. The geographers believed that the constant sunlight would weaken the ice enough for a ship to pass through Arctic seas. Hudson also believed that to be true.

HUDSON GETS HIS CHANCE

Sometime in 1607, the Muscovy Company hired Hudson to search for a Northeast Passage to Asia. The company agreed to pay the untested explorer 130 pounds and provide him with a small, three-masted sailing ship called the *Hopewell*. Hudson was also given the funds to hire a crew of ten sailors.

Soon, Hudson would be pursuing his dream and obsession of finding a new route to Asia. The lure of certain wealth and fame blocked out any doubts or misgivings he may have had. Hudson was certain that once he recruited his crew, he would be on his way to a sure success.

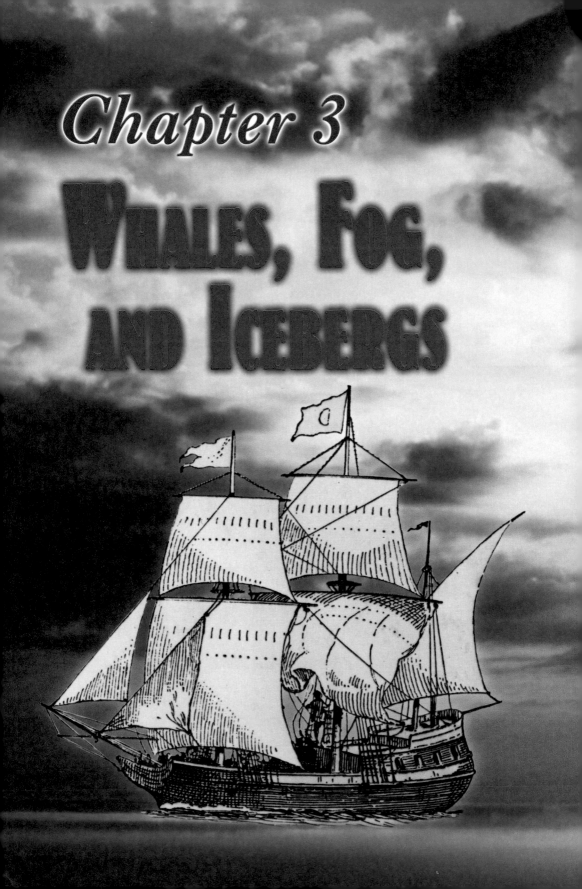

Chapter 3
Whales, Fog, and Icebergs

The Muscovy Company gave Hudson enough funds to hire a crew of ten. Hudson

added his son, John, to the crew to serve as their cabin boy. The crew that Hudson recruited was not made up of the best available sailors. The most experienced and skilled sailors did not want to sign up for a perilous voyage across uncharted Arctic waters. It is believed that the crew Hudson assembled was a band of crude, hard-drinking, petty criminals.

FOG OFF GREENLAND

In spite of the crewmen's lack of morals and ethics, Hudson persuaded his men to attend a church service with him shortly before they sailed. On April 19, 1607, Hudson and the *Hopewell*'s crew attended services at London's St. Ethelburga Church. Prayers were made for the crew to have a successful voyage and a safe return home.

Twelve days later, the *Hopewell* set sail down the Thames River toward the Atlantic Ocean. The instructions given to Hudson from the Muscovy Company were simple and precise: "Discover a passage by the North Pole to Japan and China."[1]

For about the first four weeks, the *Hopewell* followed a northerly course off the west coast of England. By late May, the ship had passed the Shetland Islands north of Scotland and all was well. The weather was sunny and warm, and favorable winds filled the *Hopewell*'s sails. Hudson

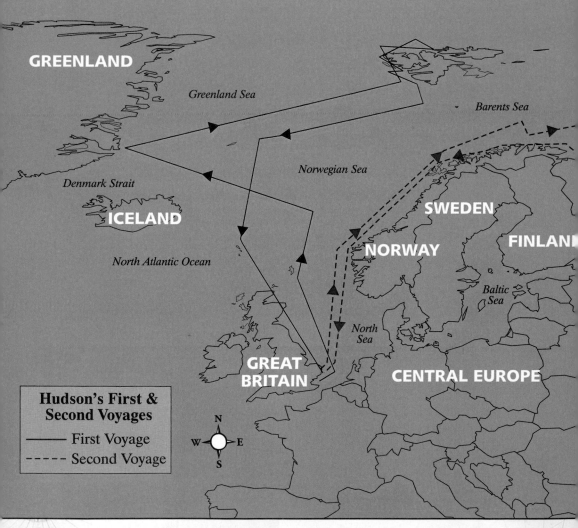

GREENLAND

Greenland Sea

Barents Sea

Denmark Strait

Norwegian Sea

ICELAND

SWEDEN

NORWAY

FINLAND

North Atlantic Ocean

Baltic Sea

North Sea

GREAT BRITAIN

CENTRAL EUROPE

Hudson's First & Second Voyages

—— First Voyage

- - - - Second Voyage

N
W • E
S

This map shows Hudson's first and second voyages. By following these routes, the explorer was trying to find the Northeast Passage.

and his crew sailed past the Faroe Islands, then past Iceland as they proceeded in a northwesterly direction.

But by early June, the sun had disappeared, and gale winds had begun blowing in from the east. The strong winds brought in fog and freezing weather. Visibility was greatly reduced, so the *Hopewell* cautiously kept close to the coast of Greenland. For brief periods, the fog would lift, and the ship's lookout could catch a hazy glimpse of land. The freezing weather made working on the ship's deck difficult and dangerous.

In a journal entry dated June 13, crewman John Pleyce glumly noted how the miserable weather conditions were making the journey difficult. "Our sails and shroud are frozen. At eight in the morning it cleared up, and the wind was out of the northeast by east, but it was so strong that we were hardly able to maintain any sail. . . . It rained all that afternoon and evening."[2]

During the foggy, rainy month of June, the *Hopewell* stayed close to the coast of Greenland. At one point, Hudson thought he had discovered a new landmass which he called Hold-with-Hope. The name reflected Hudson's belief that the climate would improve and the seas would become warmer when they reached the North Pole.

Henry Hudson spotted whales near Spitsbergen. His sighting helped the Muscovy Company establish a whaling industry.

A Brief Visit to Spitsbergen

On June 27, the *Hopewell* reached Spitsbergen, an island east of Greenland and north of Norway. While in that area, Hudson made a study of the island's coast and noted where whales could be found in great numbers. Hudson's observations would later help to establish the whaling industry in England.

While at Spitsbergen, four of Hudson's crewmen explored the island. They found much driftwood on the shore and used it for making repairs to the *Hopewell*. They also found a couple of freshwater streams, but they lacked the means for bringing back the water for their fellow crew members. While the four were onshore, the weather turned stormy, and they had to end their explorations quickly.

The return of stormy weather forced them to leave Spitsbergen and sail northeast.

Hudson was finding that the weather was steadily worsening.

The dense fog was becoming even thicker. There was more rain, colder temperatures, and stronger winds. As the voyage continued, the crew became more restless and short-tempered.

A Close Call

Along with the brutal weather conditions, large ice floes were threatening to end the voyage.

During a fierce storm, an iceberg loomed in front of Hudson and his crew. If the *Hopewell* crashed into the iceberg, it would likely sink the ship.

July 27 started off normally. The air was foggy, the waters were calm, and a light breeze blew from the east. Around midmorning, the sea started churning, and waves rose higher than the deck of the *Hopewell*. Then the crew was startled by a loud, thunderous noise. They gathered on the deck and saw a giant iceberg blocking their path. The sea pushed their ship toward the iceberg.

Hudson ordered that the ship's boat be lowered into the stormy waters. Any crewman who could handle an oar was to board the boat. A towrope was tied between the two craft. Hudson hoped that the rowboat could move the *Hopewell* out of harm's way.

The crewmen gamely tried to row the oars while crashing waves battered the small boat. It was a futile effort, but an unexpected shift in the wind moved them away from danger. The wind lasted until around noon. By that time, the *Hopewell* had safely traveled twelve miles away from the iceberg.

The *Hopewell*'s official log of the journey described the narrow escape as an act of God:

> The sea was pushing us westward toward the ice. We lowered our ship's boat and rowed to try to tow us away from the danger, which was of little use because the seas were so high; but in this menace it pleased God to give us [a] small gale from the northwest by west, and we steered away southeast for twelve miles, until noon. . . . If not

for the deliverance by God of a northwest by west wind—a wind not commonly found on this voyage—it would have been the end of us and our voyage.[3]

A ROCKY VOYAGE COMES TO AN END

The combination of a narrow escape, the miserable weather, and the continuing presence of huge ice floes probably convinced Hudson to head back to England. There is also a possibility that the crew changed Hudson's mind for him. They may have been unwilling to endure the harsh conditions any longer.

Perhaps a passage could be found at another time but not on this voyage. On July 30, Hudson wrote in the *Hopewell*'s log: "Then having a strong wind against us, and finding the fog more thick and troublesome than before, as well as the lack of various and necessary things, and not having much time left to do further good this year; I commanded our return for England."[4]

On August 15, the *Hopewell* made a brief rest stop at the Faroe Islands. After the crew refilled the water supply, the ship proceeded southward. The arduous voyage ended when the *Hopewell* docked in London on September 15.

Hudson considered the voyage a failure, but it was a success in ways that he failed to consider.

Hudson had sailed closer to the North Pole than any explorer before him. The *Hopewell* came to within six hundred miles of the pole. The maps that he sketched would greatly aid other explorers, geographers, and navigators. His first voyage also refuted the theory that the constant summer sunlight would greatly heat the waters around the North Pole.

Hudson could also report to the Muscovy Company that a direct route to Asia by way of the North Pole was not possible. The Muscovy Company would no longer have to pursue a route that did not exist. That saved the company much money. Now the traders could concentrate on pursuing other, more promising routes.

Probably the most significant accomplishment of Hudson's first voyage was his news of great pods of whales around Spitsbergen. Until that time, most of the whaling in the Atlantic had been done by Spain and France. Whaling was a profitable industry because the bones and blubber of whales had several commercial uses. Hudson's news led the Muscovy Company to sponsor fleets of whaling ships.

The members of the Muscovy Company thought that Hudson deserved another chance. They still believed that an uncharted Northeast or Northwest Passage to Asia existed. They agreed to sponsor Hudson for a second voyage.

Chapter 4

An Unhappy Crew

As the spring of 1608 neared, Hudson made plans and preparations for his second voyage. Hudson's ship and the mission were unchanged. Once again, Hudson would command the *Hopewell* and once again, he would search for a shortcut to Asia. But on the second voyage, there was a major difference in his route.

This time, Hudson would search for a passage by sailing northeast around Norway and then northward past the Russian islands of Novaya Zemlya. He hoped to find a passage north of those islands or through them, which would take him to the Kara Sea. Hudson believed that if he found the passage, then he could sail east along the Russian coastline and on to the Pacific Ocean.

If no passage could be found there, Hudson had a backup plan. According to legend, the River Ob offered a passage to Asia. The river flowed into the Kara Sea from Russia's northern shore, which was east of Novaya Zemlya. There were rumors that the sea beyond the River Ob was warm and could be crossed easily.

ONE PARTICULAR TROUBLEMAKER

On April 22, 1608, the *Hopewell* sailed from St. Katherine's Docks in London. There was a slightly larger crew, fifteen sailors compared to twelve (including Hudson and his son) on the first voyage. Except for Hudson's son, John, none of the crew members from the first voyage opted to sail with Hudson a second time.

One of the new crew members, Robert Juet, would emerge as a troublemaker. Juet was an ill-tempered and spiteful man who disliked taking orders. In spite of Juet's character flaws, Hudson chose him to serve as his first mate, or second in command. Hudson biographer Llewelyn Powys writes that Juet was "cynical, skeptical and dangerous."[1] However, Juet was an experienced navigator, and that may have caused Hudson to overlook his flaws.

AN ICY JOURNEY

The voyage got off to a bad start. Freezing cold and fog plagued the *Hopewell*. The harsh weather affected the crew badly. On May 25, Hudson wrote in the ship's log: "[T]he cold began on the twenty-first, at which time my carpenter became sick and still is. Three or four of my crew are also becoming sick, I suppose due to the cold."[2]

In early June, the *Hopewell* began running into ice. Hudson decided that the ship could work its way through the obstacle instead of going around it. That was a costly and near-fatal mistake. The ship's log notes that on June 9 from noon to four, the *Hopewell* futilely tried to go through the ice. Hudson had nearly sent the ship into an icy impasse. He admitted his mistake by writing, "By this time, we were so far in, 12 to 15 miles, and the ice so thick and firm ahead, that we had endangered ourselves; we returned the way that we had entered, suffering only a few rubs of the ship against the ice. By eight o'clock this evening, we got free of it."[3]

For the following week, ice to the north and east of the *Hopewell* slowed the ship. The frigid weather froze the rigging of the ship and made it very difficult for the crew to man the sails.

Men Claim to See a Mermaid

The freezing weather and lack of mobility may have caused some of the crew to hallucinate. On June 15, two crew members reported that they sighted a mermaid. Crewmen Thomas Hilles and Robert Rayner claimed that they spotted the mythical sea creature on the morning of June 15. Hudson made note of this incredible incident in the ship's log:

This morning, one of our company looking overboard saw a mermaid and calling up some of the company to come see her one more came up, and by that time she was come close to the ship's side, looking earnestly on the men; a little after the sea came and overturned her; from the navil upwards her back and breasts were like a woman's, as they say that saw her; her body was as big as one of us; her skin very white, and long hair hanging down behind, of color black. In her going down they saw her tail, which was like the tail of a porpoise, and speckled like a mackerel.[4]

A reported sighting of such an enchanting creature was just a temporary respite from the repeated attempts to break through the engulfing ice floes. Hudson finally realized he had to try

Many seamen often claimed they saw mermaids swimming through the choppy waves of the Atlantic Ocean.

something new. He reluctantly turned his ship southward. His new plan was to sail down the coast of Novaya Zemlya to find a passage through the island that lead into the Kara Sea.

A Bountiful Island

By late June, the *Hopewell* was in calm waters a couple of miles off the coast of Novaya Zemlya. Hudson ordered Juet and his boatswain, Thomas Cooke, to lead four other crew members to explore the island and replenish the ship's supply of fresh water.

The men returned bearing deer horns and whale fins. They reported seeing tracks of foxes, deer, and bears in the melting snow. The men also reported seeing grass and streams formed by melting snow. While returning to the *Hopewell,* their small boat was followed by large herds of walrus.

The news of walruses encouraged Hudson. He knew that the large sea mammals were more active and prevalent in warm currents. Maybe they could lead him to the warm water passage he sought. He tried tracking them, but he could not learn anything from where they were migrating.

Ironically, there was a wide strait due south of the islands, which led to the Kara Sea. Since it was undiscovered, none of the maps at that time showed it. Hudson continued to sail down the

Hudson explored the icy coast of Novaya Zemlya. This map of the islands was made in the 1600s.

De eylande van Orange

C. de troost

C. de Nassow

Het behouden Huys

Heemskerd hoeck

Cruys Eylandt

Willems Eylandt

Beerefoort

Den Swarten hoeck

D'Admiraliteyts Eylandt

NOVA ZEMBLA

Tartariæ Pars

say aven

Eylandt

et laeghe landt

Twe Eylanden

State Eylandt

Oby fl.

Weygats

Deton hoeck

Valcken hoeck

IAE PARS

western coast of the islands to look for a way through them.

AN APPROACHING ICEBERG

On July 2, a river was spotted, and Hudson decided to see where it led. His decision nearly had tragic results. As the *Hopewell* turned into the river, Hudson and his crew sighted a large iceberg coming from the south. The iceberg was headed directly toward the ship.

They didn't have time to hoist their sails and escape. Hudson quickly ordered the entire crew to one side of the ship. The crewmen used beams, oars, and poles to push and poke at the iceberg. They worked all day at warding off the iceberg. At around six in the evening, they were finally out of harm's way.

In the ship's log, Hudson called the iceberg "very fearfull to looke on" and gave thanks to God for helping to free them from danger and disaster.[5] "But by the mercy of God and his mightie helpe . . . we escaped the danger," Hudson wrote.[6]

After that narrow escape, Hudson sent Juet and five other crew members out on a boat to explore the river. They returned with some disappointing news. After going between eighteen and twenty-four miles upriver, they found that the river became too shallow to navigate any farther. Hudson glumly noted that "had this sound held

This is an arctic iceberg, much like the one Hudson and his crew encountered.

as it did make good show of for depth, breadth, safeness of harbor, and good anchor ground, it might have yielded an excellent passage to a more easterly sea."[7]

As the *Hopewell* sailed on, Hudson found that the seas were becoming even more clogged with ice. He reluctantly acknowledged that his second voyage would also be a failure. On July 5, Hudson documented his continued failure by writing, "I suppose that there will be no navigable passage this way."[8]

For the second time in two years, he would have to tell the Muscovy Company that his voyage had been in vain. But this time it would be even more difficult. After the first voyage, his report on the pods of whales ultimately helped the Muscovy Company make money in the whaling industry. This time, there would be no reports of a potentially profitable enterprise.

⬤ THE CREW FORCES HUDSON TO TURN BACK

Yet Hudson did not immediately give up. Instead of sailing south toward England, he took the *Hopewell* in a westerly direction. He was headed toward North America before his crew changed his mind. It is believed that Juet was going to incite a mutiny if Hudson did not return the *Hopewell* to England.

According to the ship's log, Hudson made the decision without being coerced by the crew. Historians believe that Hudson's rebellious crew forced him to write that statement so they would avoid being punished for mutiny. At that time, committing mutiny was a hanging offense.

The entry Hudson made in the ship's log on August 7 reads, "I used all my diligence to arrive at London, and therefore now I gave my companie a certificate under my hand, of my free and willing return, without persuasion or force by any one or more of them."[9]

On August 26, the *Hopewell* docked at Gravesend, England, which was twenty-two miles from London. Hudson returned with some detailed maps that would be very useful to geographers. But he failed to bring back anything of economic benefit to the Muscovy Company.

Hudson still believed that a passage existed and could be found. He hoped the Muscovy Company would finance a third voyage, but the company was no longer interested in backing someone who had failed twice. Hudson would have to look outside of England for a new sponsor.

Chapter 5

Fighting to Sail Again

In the fall of 1608, Henry Hudson was a captain without a ship and an explorer without a sponsor. The directors of the Muscovy Company were thoroughly disappointed after his second voyage failed to find a shortcut to Asia.

Yet Hudson was not discouraged. He still believed in his abilities even if the directors of the Muscovy Company no longer did. His two Arctic voyages had earned him a reputation as a courageous and skilled navigator. There were still merchants interested in finding the yet undiscovered passage. It would not take Hudson long to find a new sponsor.

THE POLITICAL SITUATION

At that time, the Netherlands was about to win its independence from Spain. Since the 1300s, Spain had ruled the European nations known as the Low Countries (the Netherlands, Belgium, and Luxembourg). But in the 1500s, a Protestant religious movement known as the Reformation spread through the Low Countries. Spanish kings Charles V and Philip II tried to suppress the movement by persecuting Protestants. That led to a rebellion against Spanish rule.

In 1581, a confederation of northern provinces declared their independence from Spain. The confederation would later become known as the Dutch Republic or the Netherlands. The Dutch battled Spain for their freedom and, in 1609, Spain signed a treaty recognizing the Dutch nation's independence.

While the Dutch were fighting the Spanish, Dutch merchants were aggressively competing with the English for foreign trade. In 1602, they founded the Dutch East India Company (DEIC). It was a large, well-financed organization with more money than the Muscovy Company. The DEIC owned a fleet of forty large vessels—and a large number of smaller ones that employed around five thousand sailors.

A MEETING WITH THE DUTCH

While Hudson remained in London looking for a new sponsor, he was contacted by Edward van Meteren, a Dutch government official. Van Meteren arranged for Hudson to travel to Amsterdam to meet with the directors of the Dutch East India Company.

While staying in the Netherlands, Hudson stayed with Peter Plancius, who was the official cartographer for the DEIC. Hudson and Plancius studied maps and charts and discussed the possibility of finding a new route to Asia. Hudson visited with Jodocus Hondius, a well-respected cartographer as well. Plancius and Hondius became friends and allies of Hudson. They would help to persuade the DEIC to sponsor Hudson on his third voyage.

When Hudson first met with the directors of the DEIC, they were not unanimous in their support. Hudson proposed to follow a route that was very similar to the one he used on his second voyage. Hudson told them that the major difference was that there would be no turning back during the third voyage. He said that he would not quit until the elusive passage was finally found.

While Hudson's passion and self-assurance impressed the directors, there were still some skeptics. There was enough opposition to get Hudson's supporters to rethink their position. The directors informed Hudson that they could not agree to back him until they met again in March 1609. But even if they approved another voyage, a ship and crew would not be ready until 1610. The DEIC paid Hudson for his travel expenses and sent him on his way.

HUDSON IS OFFERED A THIRD VOYAGE

Hudson was disappointed, but he refused to give up this voyage. He decided to stay in Amsterdam a while longer and continue to meet with Plancius.

Henry Hudson meeting with the directors of the Dutch East India Company to discuss his plans to search for a northeast passage on his third voyage.

Hudson drew a map for Plancius, showing areas of the North American coast that could lead to the short passage he sought. Hudson had received a letter and some maps from his friend, Captain John Smith, who had been one of the founders of the new colony in Jamestown, Virginia.

Smith had the mistaken idea that the North American continent was a few hundred miles wide. He had suggested to Hudson that a sea route to Asia could be found somewhere north of Virginia. Plancius was unconvinced, but he still felt that it was possible.

While Hudson and Plancius were studying maps and pondering routes, King Henry IV of France told his ambassador to the Netherlands to meet with Hudson. France had set up a few colonies in Canada, but they were not nearly as profitable as the foreign trade that England and the Netherlands were conducting. Finding a short passage to Asia could be immensely profitable for the French.

Hudson had a series of secret interviews with the French ambassador, Pierre Jeannin. Hudson did not care whose flag he sailed under as long as he could find a sponsor. Somehow, the Amsterdam directors of the DEIC learned about the secret talks between Hudson and Jeannin. The threat of losing Hudson's services got the directors to offer Hudson a contract.

In late December, the directors drew up a contract. Hudson signed it on January 8, 1609. That settled things for Hudson. There would be a third voyage, and he would be working for the Dutch instead of the French.

The terms of the contract were precise and, for Hudson, a bit restrictive. The directors were convinced that the short route to Asia lay to the northeast. By signing the contract, Hudson agreed to forego looking for a Northwest Passage. The contract read: "Hudson shall about the first of April, sail, in order to search for a passage by the north around the north side of Nova Zembla, and shall continue thus along that parallel until he shall be able to sail southward to a latitude of 60 degrees."[1]

Shortly before Hudson sailed, the contract was amended to guarantee that he would not go off looking for another route. The amended contract clearly stated that Hudson was not allowed "to think of discovering no other route or passage, except the route around the north or northeast, above Nova Zembla. . . . If it could not be accomplished at that time, another route would be subject of consideration for another voyage."[2]

Hudson further agreed to return to the directors "his journals, log-books and charts, together with an account of everything whatsoever which

shall happen to him during the voyage, without keeping anything back."[3]

For agreeing to their terms, Hudson would be paid eight hundred Dutch guilders, which was not a large amount of money at that time. If he failed to return in a year, Hudson's wife would receive an additional two hundred guilders. If Hudson was successful in his quest, he would have to move his family to the Netherlands. He would also be prohibited from working for anyone except the DEIC.

It is not known if Hudson planned to violate the contract. When he signed it, he may have intended to honor its terms. But information that he received after the signing would lead him to make his own plans.

THE CREW OF THE HALF MOON

For about the next three months, Hudson busied himself with finding a ship, recruiting a crew, and acquiring all the provisions needed for the long voyage. From the DEIC's large fleet, Hudson was given a ship called the *Half Moon*. By today's standards, it would be considered a small ship. The *Half Moon* weighed around eighty tons and was about sixty feet long. At its widest point, it measured about sixteen feet across.

When Hudson first saw the *Half Moon*, he could see that it was seaworthy. Although small, it was well built, and its wood was treated to endure and withstand the rough, cold seas. Unfortunately, the *Half Moon* would serve Hudson better than the crew he signed up.

Since he did not speak Dutch, Hudson preferred to command an all-English crew. That would prevent communication problems. But the DEIC insisted upon a mixture of English and Dutch sailors. Hudson's first mate and at least half of the crew had to be Dutch sailors.

Hudson was able to take along some experienced English sailors from his earlier voyages. His son, John, would accompany his father again. John Colman from Hudson's first voyage and Robert Juet, a veteran of the second voyage, were members of the *Half Moon*'s crew. Hudson's selection of Juet was a puzzling one. Perhaps he believed that Juet's experience and skills outweighed his potential to cause problems.

On April 4 or 6, 1609, the *Half Moon* quietly left the port of Amsterdam. To the few people working or sightseeing on the docks, it looked no different from any other cargo vessel leaving the port that day. Hudson had recruited a crew variously reported as sixteen, eighteen, or twenty sailors. A few wives and girlfriends boarded the *Half Moon* to say their last farewells to the sailors.

This replica of the *Half Moon* is on display on the Hudson River near Albany, New York.

A ROUGH START

After ordering the anchor raised, Hudson skillfully navigated the *Half Moon* through the crowded harbor. About two days later, the *Half Moon* cleared the island of Texel in the North Sea. From there, the ship proceeded up the coast of Norway toward the Arctic Ocean.

As the *Half Moon* sailed north, the crew became more short-tempered and unruly. Arguments and fistfights became regular occurrences. The Dutch sailors had a difficult time. They were not used to the cold temperatures. They had been more accustomed to Pacific voyages with warm waters and bright sunshine. Now they were trying to cope with ice, fog, and stormy seas.

In early May, the *Half Moon* passed the North Cape of Norway and entered the ice-strewn waters of the Arctic Ocean. Dismay, if not despair, set in when the crew found the waters blocked by gigantic ice floes. Their ship was hemmed in, unable to move to the north or the south. After a month of sailing, they were stuck in the ice with nowhere to go.

Historians believe that the insufferable conditions led the crew to stage a mutiny. Historians also believe that Juet took an active part in it. Dutch historian, Emanuel Van Meteren, had access to the *Half Moon*'s records and may have spoken to Hudson about his third voyage. According to Van Meteren, the Dutch sailors sparked the mutiny by refusing to sail farther north.

Hudson had a record of backing down when his crew rebelled. He wanted to ignore the terms of his contract. Hudson wanted to explore North America for a Northwest Passage to Asia. Van Meteren claims that Hudson offered his crew two westerly options. It is not known which one they chose, but Hudson's offer quelled the mutiny.

Hudson issued new orders. The *Half Moon* turned westward. On May 19, it passed the North Cape of Norway for the second time. Hudson and his crew now looked to the west with renewed hope and resolve to find the fabled passage.

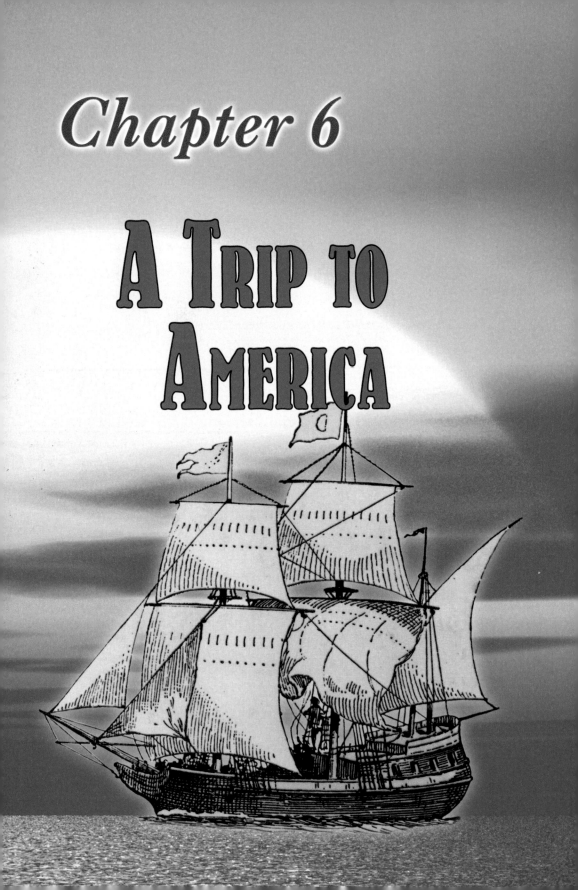

Chapter 6

A Trip to America

The *Half Moon*'s new course got off to a shaky start when the ship was struck by a violent storm in late May. The ship was sailing by the Lofoten Islands when the storm hit. Pounding and punishing winds from the northeast rocked the ship for twenty-four hours. In the ship's log, Juet described the storm: "It blew so vehemently and the sea went so high, and brake withal that it would have endangered a small ship to lie under the seas, so we scudded seventy leagues in four and twenty hours. The storm began to cease at four of the clock."[1]

When the storm ended, the *Half Moon* was still on its course for North America. It was a tribute to both Hudson's great navigational skills and the ship's seaworthiness. Hudson and his crew survived a violent storm without a loss of life, provisions, or sails. Surviving the ordeal must have been considered an omen that they would succeed on this voyage.

After a one-day stop at the Faroe Islands to replenish its water supplies, the *Half Moon* ran into another vicious storm. This time, damage was unavoidable. The foremast was lost when it was swept overboard. The ship also suffered some damage to its deck, but it stayed on course.

On July 2, the lookout on the *Half Moon* sighted land, the Grand Banks of Newfoundland. As the ship headed for the shoreline the crew saw a fleet of French fishing boats. Hudson decided to steer clear of the boats. He had a route to follow and a broken mast to repair.

The *Half Moon* traveled slowly southward. On occasional days, there was no wind. The crew passed the time fishing. Juet noted that on July 8, they hauled in a catch of 118 cod and sighted many big schools of herring. Four days later, they spotted land and prepared to approach it. But a thick fog descended over the ship. They were forced to drop anchor and wait for the fog to lift.

ATTACK ON THE INDIANS

For the next three days, the *Half Moon* remained motionless. On the fourth day of their wait, the fog lifted. Hudson and his crew docked near what is now Penobscot Bay in Maine. Before anyone could go ashore, two canoes with six American Indians approached the ship. This was Hudson's first encounter with American Indians, and he was wary of them.

The American Indians came in friendship. This was not their first encounter with white people. They wanted to trade, and Hudson gave them a

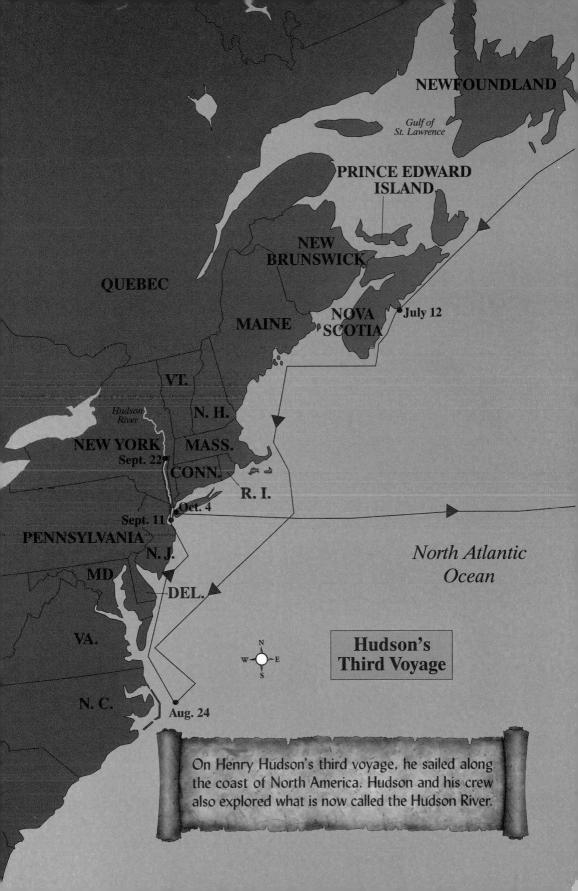

NEWFOUNDLAND

Gulf of St. Lawrence

PRINCE EDWARD ISLAND

QUEBEC

NEW BRUNSWICK

NOVA SCOTIA

MAINE

July 12

VT.

Hudson River

N. H.

NEW YORK

Sept. 22

MASS.

CONN.

R. I.

Oct. 4

Sept. 11

PENNSYLVANIA

N. J.

MD

DEL.

VA.

N. C.

Aug. 24

North Atlantic Ocean

N
W   E
S

Hudson's Third Voyage

On Henry Hudson's third voyage, he sailed along the coast of North America. Hudson and his crew also explored what is now called the Hudson River.

few trinkets along with some food and drink. In return, they offered some information about silver, copper, and gold mines that could be found on shore.

Actually, the mines did not exist. The Indians may have said that in hopes of getting Hudson and his crew to give them some more gifts.

Hudson's crewmen were suspicious of the Indians and their intentions. The crewmen believed

Hudson and his crew met American Indians on their third voyage.

that the Indians might harm or even kill them. Crew members decided to attack the Indians before the Indians could do the sailors any harm. On July 25, six crew members armed themselves with muskets and other weapons, boarded a row-boat, and stole a boat from the Indians. They brought the stolen boat back to the *Half Moon*.

Later that day, twelve crew members took a boat to where the Indians were camped. In the ship's log, Juet wrote that they "drove the savages from their houses and took the spoil of them as they would have done of us."[2]

Hudson went along with his crew's behavior. No one was punished. As one Hudson biographer notes, "That Hudson . . . should have consented to such an evil is extraordinary, and can only confirm us in our belief that through some inherent weak-ness of character he was incapable of keeping his insubordinate crew under control."[3]

SEARCHING THE COAST

Fearing a revenge attack, Hudson ordered the crew to prepare for an early departure. At 5 A.M. the following morning, the *Half Moon* cast off and headed south. A week later, the ship anchored off the shore of Cape Cod in present day Massachu-setts. Hudson sent a few crewmen ashore to explore the land. They returned with a bounty of grapes and rose trees.

As the ship continued south, the summer days got longer and hotter, and the crewmen's tempers became shorter. Hudson was becoming worried and doubtful. What if no passage could be found? If that happened, Hudson would return to Europe with news of a third unsuccessful voyage.

By mid-August, the *Half Moon* was off the coast of Virginia, a short distance from Jamestown. Hudson's friend John Smith was in Jamestown at that time, but Hudson made no effort to contact him. Historians are still puzzled by Hudson's behavior. Several explanations have been given.

Perhaps Hudson was trying to hide his association with Smith. Since he was sailing under a Dutch flag, Hudson may have wanted to avoid visiting an English colony. Maybe Hudson was simply obsessed with finding the undiscovered passage and a visit would only have have been a distraction.

Whatever the reason, on August 19 the *Half Moon* turned around and went north. Hudson took the ship into the Chesapeake Bay and then the Delaware Bay. Both times, Hudson found that these rivers were too shallow and small to lead to the Pacific Ocean. On September 3, the *Half Moon* sailed past the southern coast of Staten Island, New York. This time, they spotted three large rivers. Hudson decided to explore the largest of the three.

At the Mouth of a Great River

As they neared the entrance of the largest river, Hudson had some crewmen go out in the ship's boat to take some soundings. After they reported that it was deep enough, Hudson ordered his ship to proceed.

When the *Half Moon* slowly proceeded forward, Hudson and his crew marveled at the marine life. After some crewmen went ashore with a fishing net, Juet reported that they caught "ten great mullets, of a foot-and-a-half apiece and a ray so great as four men could haul into the ship."[4]

The following day, Hudson and his crew were greeted by some Indians who gave them some tobacco, which was exchanged for some knives and beads. In his journal, Hudson described their dress, food, weapons, and homes:

> Their clothing consisted of the skin of foxes and other animals, which they dress and make the skins into garments of various sorts. Their food is Turkish wheat [maize or Indian corn], whey they cook by baking, and it is excellent eating. . . . their weapons are bows and arrows, pointed with sharp stones, which they fasten with hard resin. They had no houses, but slept under the blue heavens, sometimes on mats of bulrushes, interwoven, and sometimes on the leaves of trees.[5]

A few of the visitors spent the entire day aboard the *Half Moon* and thoroughly examined every nook and cranny of the vessel. The whole time, Hudson and his crewmen kept a watchful eye on their guests. Juet wrote that "we durst not [don't dare to] trust them."[6]

In his journal, Hudson made it clear that he distrusted the Indians and thought that most of them were just thieves: "They appear to be a friendly people, but have a great propensity to steal, and are exceedingly adroit in carrying away whatever they take a fancy to."[7]

On September 12, 1609, Hudson arrived at the mouth of what would be known as the Hudson River.

⊕A Frightening Night

The next day, Hudson's distrust became well founded. Hudson sent John Colman and four other crewmen off in a rowboat to measure the water's depth. The trip began pleasantly. The men admired the new scenery of grass, flowers, and trees while enjoying the "very sweet smells [that] came from them."[8]

Their hopes of finding a passage were buoyed when they came upon "an open sea" which is now called New York Harbor.[9] They turned the rowboat around and headed back to their ship. They were eager to tell Hudson the good news.

Suddenly, Indians attacked them in two canoes. According to Hudson's journal, one canoe contained twelve men and the second canoe carried fourteen. The attackers launched a barrage of arrows. The crewmen started rowing furiously to get out of the arrows' range. They were armed and ready to return the Indians' fire, but rain and darkness thwarted them.

The darkness prevented them from aiming their firearms at their attackers. The rain snuffed out the fuse they needed to light their gunpowder. They had no way to fight back. Colman died after being shot in the throat by an arrow. Two other crewmen were seriously wounded.

The frightened survivors rowed around the waters aimlessly hoping to find their ship. They were not able to locate the *Half Moon* until the next morning. Colman was buried at a place Hudson named Colman's Point in his honor.

MORE TROUBLE WITH INDIANS

Despite the attack, Hudson and his crew continued to trade with the Indians, although Hudson fortified the ship. The crew boarded up the portholes and armed guards patrolled the deck. Hudson stationed a lookout in the crow's nest, and the crew loaded and readied the ship's cannon for firing.

The uneasy peace with the Indians ended on September 9. The Indians rowed two large canoes to the *Half Moon* to trade. When one group came on board armed with bows and arrows, Hudson's crewmen seized two Indians and held them captive. One Indian escaped by jumping overboard. The other was set free when he appeared to show no hostility toward the crew.

In his journal, Hudson again makes it clear that he expected the Indians to steal from them: "In the morning two great canoes full of men came aboard, one armed with bows and arrows, the other, in an attempt to deceive us, pretended interest in buying knives. But we were aware of their intent and took two of them as prisoners."[10]

The following day, the *Half Moon* sailed up the New York River, which would later bear Hudson's

Although he had some bad relations with American Indians, Henry Hudson did trade with the Indians on Manhattan Island at the beginning of his journey up the Hudson River. This wood engraving is from 1876.

name. Their small rowboat moved ahead of the ship and constantly tested the depth of the water with a weighted line. On September 11, more Indians visited the *Half Moon* and bestowed gifts upon Hudson and his crew. As usual, Hudson was distrustful and questioned their motives. "The people of the country came aboard of us, making show of love, and gave us tobacco and Indian wheat, and departed for that night; but we durst [dared] not trust them."[11]

On September 12, a fleet of twenty-eight canoes greeted the *Half Moon*, but Hudson was too distrustful to allow any Indians to board his ship. He did buy some oysters and beans from them, however.

MAKING FRIENDS

In spite of the constant fear of Indian attack, the journey up the Hudson River was a relaxing one. The *Half Moon* had to travel at a slow, leisurely pace because it was constantly waiting for the rowboat to check the river's depth. There were further delays because Indians from both shores were paddling out to look at the ship. It took the *Half Moon* two weeks to travel from the southern tip of Manhattan to an area where the city of Albany, New York, now stands.

As Hudson progressed northward, his relations with the Indians became more amicable. At times,

Hudson and his crewmen would go ashore with them. In one journal entry, Hudson wrote of a pleasant visit. He went ashore in a canoe with a tribal chief who proved to be a gracious host. Hudson marveled at the sturdy construction of the chief's oak bark house and at the abundance of corn and beans that the Indians had stored.

Hudson was treated to a dinner of pigeons and dog and was asked to spend the evening. When he politely declined, the Indians assured him of their good intentions by destroying their arrows. That made a long lasting impression on Hudson. "The natives are a very good people," he wrote in the ship's log, "for when they saw that I would

Even when American Indians welcomed him, Henry Hudson was unsure of whether or not to trust them. This was in part due to his men mistreating the Indians at different points of the *Half Moon's* journey.

not remain, they supposed that I was afraid of their bows, and taking the arrows, they broke them in pieces and threw them in the fire."[12]

MORE BLOOD IS SHED

But as his journey up the river continued, Hudson became more fretful and less confident. The scenery of towering trees and majestic mountains could not keep him from thinking that his third voyage could end in failure. Hudson's worst fears were confirmed on September 22 when the rowboat crew reported that they could go no farther.

The rowboat had journeyed up a smaller river, and found that the water was only seven feet deep. The next day, Hudson glumly turned the *Half Moon* southward. Hudson was disappointed because he once again failed to find the short passage to Asia. The crewmen were disappointed because they expected to become wealthy and famous. Their frustration and disappointment made them resentful and edgy.

On October 1, some Indians were aboard the *Half Moon* trading furs and tobacco. One of them wandered off and entered Juet's cabin. Two shirts, two ammunition belts, and a pillow were stolen. The theft was discovered quickly before the thief could return to his canoe. Without hesitating, a crewman shot and killed the thief. The sound of

The American Indians of the Hudson River would often paddle out to the *Half Moon* to trade with Henry Hudson and the other members of his crew.

the gunshot caused the other Indians aboard to leave the ship quickly.

A few of the crewmen boarded the rowboat and pursued the fleeing Indians. One Indian swam out to the rowboat and tried to capsize it. The ship's cook chopped off the Indian's hand with a sword. After ending the chase, the crewmen rowed back to the *Half Moon*. Hudson ordered them to lift anchor. They escaped.

At daybreak on October 2, a small army of Indians in canoes began chasing and firing arrows at the *Half Moon*. Juet described the skirmish by writing:

> Two canoes full of men, with their bows and arrows shot at us after our stern: in recompense whereof we discharged six muskets and killed two or three of them. Then about a hundred of them came to [a] point of land to shoot at us. There I shot a falcon [light cannon] at them and killed two of them: whereupon the rest fled into the woods. Yet they manned off another canoe with by nine or ten men, which came to meet us. So I shot at it also with a falcon, and shot it through and killed one of them. Then our men with their muskets killed three or four more of them. So they went their way.[13]

AN UNHAPPY EMPLOYER

On October 4, the *Half Moon* was back on the open sea. It docked at Dartmouth, England, on

November 7, 1609. Hudson quickly wrote a report that he sent to the DEIC along with the charts, maps, and logs of his third voyage. In his report, Hudson asked the DEIC to sponsor another voyage to begin on March 1, 1610. He proposed that his new ship could work as a whaler during April and May. That would help the voyage pay for itself.

It took several weeks for Hudson's report to reach the DEIC officials in Amsterdam. Windy conditions delayed the ship carrying the letter from crossing the English Channel. When the DEIC officials read Hudson's letter, they were very displeased. They would not even talk about financing a new voyage until he returned the *Half Moon* to Amsterdam.

That is when a major problem arose. English authorities refused to allow Hudson and his English crewmen to leave their country. Hudson was further ordered to end all communication with the DEIC. For the time being, Hudson had nowhere to go and no hope of going on another voyage.

Chapter 7

The Last Voyage

In the early 1600s, England became resentful and jealous over Holland's success in expanding its foreign trade activities. To English merchants, Hudson's latest voyage was yet another example of the Dutch trying to expand their political and economic influence. Hudson had become a pawn in a political power struggle.

Holland tried to broker a diplomatic solution to Hudson's situation. Their ambassador and the English ambassador exchanged notes. England stood firm and refused to release Hudson.

In July 1610, the English permitted the *Half Moon* and some of its Dutch crewmen to return to Amsterdam. Still, Hudson was not allowed to leave England or communicate with the DEIC. Apparently, the only way Hudson could get out of England was by going on another voyage, so that was what he did.

THE FURIOUS OVERFALL

Hudson had failed to find a Northeast Passage on his first voyage. The Dutch had hired him to explore that area again, but he opted to explore North America. He failed to

find a Northwest Passage along the coast of that continent. However, there was one unexplored route in a corner of the North Atlantic that held some promise.

From 1585 to 1588, an English explorer and navigator, John Davis, explored a huge strait between Greenland and Canada that bears his name. Davis discovered an area of roaring and swirling water that he called the Furious Overfall. Davis believed that the overfall offered a gateway to a still undiscovered Northwest Passage. Davis described the Furious Overfall: "We fell into a mighty race, where an island of ice was carried by the force of the current as fast as our barke could sail. We saw the sea falling down into a gulfe with a mighty overfal, and moving with divers circular motions like whirlpooles, in such sort as forcible streams passe thorow the arches of bridges."[1]

Hudson had wanted to explore that route during his second voyage before the threat of a mutiny changed his plans. During that voyage he wrote in his journal, "Considering the time and means that we had, if the wind should be favorable to us, as it had during the first part of our voyage, I would try for that place called Lumley's Inlet, and Captain John Davis's Furious Overfall."[2]

In that journal entry, Hudson wisely omitted mentioning the threat of a mutiny. He claimed that he thought it more important to conserve their dwindling resources by returning to England. He wrote that doing otherwise would be "giving way to foolish rashness and wasted time."[3]

A New Ship and More Troublesome Crewmen

Several influential and wealthy London merchants were still eager to sponsor Hudson for a voyage through the Furious Overfall. Sir Thomas Smith, Sir Dudley Digges, and John Wolstenholme were his major sponsors. He received additional support from Henry Frederick, the Prince of Wales and son of English King James I.

Hudson's sponsors acted quickly to get him the ship he wanted. It was called the *Discovery*. His sponsors also permitted Hudson to chart his own course and purchase all the supplies he needed. With one unfortunate exception, Hudson was allowed to pick all of his crew.

The unfortunate exception was a sailor named Henry Greene. Greene was known to be a troublemaker and a petty criminal. Robert Juet, who would be sailing with Hudson one final time, immediately distrusted Greene. He believed that Greene had been recruited to spy on his fellow crew members. According to one Hudson biographer, Greene "belonged to the underworld, was clever, physically strong and able to turn his hand to anything."[4]

Juet would be going on his third voyage with Hudson, and Hudson had once again made him his first mate. But as one writer noted, "This mark of the captain's confidence in him would neither improve the man's disposition nor secure his loyalty."[5]

Hudson had no reason to doubt the loyalty and abilities of the rest of his twenty-one man crew. Five of them, including Hudson's son, John, had served under Hudson during his previous voyages. The others, except for Greene, had good references. They were all capable sailors who also knew how to fire guns.

QUARRELING CREW

On the afternoon of April 17, 1610, the *Discovery* began sailing up England's east coast. By May 11, it had reached Iceland. A combination of contrary winds and fog delayed further sailing. Hudson found a safe harbor to dock in, and he waited out the weather.

The unexpected delay allowed the crew to fish, hunt, and bathe in the island's hot springs. Unfortunately, it also gave them time to quarrel. Greene and Edward Wilson, the ship's surgeon, had an argument that escalated into a fight. It is believed that Greene started the fight, but Hudson sided with Greene. Hudson may have believed that Wilson started it, for he had once said that Wilson had "a tongue that would Wrong his best friend."[6] The crew sided with Wilson, and they resented their captain's actions.

Wilson was so angry that he threatened to jump ship and stay in Iceland. Somehow, he was persuaded to stay on.

A second troubling incident occurred when Juet was overheard saying that Greene was aboard to spy on the crew for Hudson. One account claims that Juet was drunk when he said it, but most of the crew believed him. Distrust and resentment of Hudson by his crew grew even stronger.

TRAPPED IN THE ICE

After the *Discovery* left Iceland, Hudson learned of what Juet had said, but did nothing to reprimand or discipline his first mate. Perhaps he was simply too busy and obsessed with charting the course for the Furious Overfall. On June 25, the *Discovery* entered the strait between Baffin Island and Quebec, Canada that today bears Hudson's name.

Traveling became more difficult for Hudson and his crew. Swift tides at the mouth of the strait sent large icebergs floating in all directions. Hudson's skillful navigating kept the ship from a fatal collision. Hudson did not know it, but if he had entered the strait in mid-July instead of late June, the trip would have been much safer. By mid-July, the tides would have been less turbulent and the icebergs would have melted.

A combination of strong currents and ice floes eventually halted the *Discovery*. Hudson steered his ship on a southerly course into Ungava Bay where it became stuck in the unyielding ice. Prickett described the icy impasse by writing: "Our course took us wherever the ice would allow, but we were always enclosed with ice. When our master saw this, he changed his course to the south, thinking in this way to clear himself of the ice: but the more he struggled, the more he became enclosed, and the worse off he was, until finally we could go no farther."[7]

By this time, most of the crew doubted Hudson's ability to command them. They were openly quarreling and becoming convinced that their captain had lost his way. Hudson responded by calling the crew together and showing them his chart. He asked the crew to decide if they wanted to proceed any farther.

According to Prickett, "Some were of one mind and some of another, some wishing themselves at home and some not caring where they were, if once out of the ice."[8] Prickett does not say what they decided. He merely writes, "Much was said to no purpose, then all hands had to get to work to clear the ship and get ourselves out of the ice."[9]

ICELAND

Denmark
Strait

May 11

GREENLAND

Baffin Bay

June 4

Baffin
Island

Davis Strait

North Atlantic
Ocean

July 28

June 25

Labrador Sea

Aug 3

July 8

Hudson's Fourth Voyage

Hudson Bay

QUEBEC

N
W   E
S

NEWFOUNDLAND

Mutiny June 22, 1611

Nov. 1, 1610 to
June 18, 1611

ONTARIO

On his fourth voyage, Henry Hudson sailed along the coasts of Iceland and Greenland. He also sailed into what is now called Hudson Bay.

The discussion was probably cut short by the impending threat of colliding with an iceberg.

Mysterious Mounds

It took Hudson and his crew three weeks to break free of the ice. The quarreling and doubting resumed, but so did the voyage. In early August, the *Discovery* passed between a pair of one thousand-foot-high headlands. Hudson named them Cape Wolstenholme and Cape Digges in honor of his two most enthusiastic sponsors.

Between the two newly named headlands, the *Discovery* entered a channel about five miles wide. Hudson likely believed that the most difficult part of their voyage was over. Surely, there was an open sea at the end of the channel, and beyond that sea lay a passage to the Pacific and Asia.

Hudson sent Greene, Prickett, and a few other crewmen to explore Digges Island. They found a herd of deer and many wild fowl. The crewmen were puzzled by the presence of several stone mounds that appeared to be made by humans. Prickett examined one of them and found it full of wild fowls hanging by their necks. The Inuit had probably built the mound as a storage place.

A Futile Search

After the crewmen returned to their ship, they urged Hudson to stay for a few more days. That would give them some extra time to explore this newly discovered island of plenty. Hudson refused the crewmen's request. He was eager to find the passage that he believed must be so near. He was confident that they could find another place to replenish their provisions.

For the next few weeks, the *Discovery* sailed a southerly course down the east side of the huge bay now named for Hudson. For a time, the crew was quiet and compliant. But things started coming apart after Hudson steered the *Discovery* into James Bay. Hudson wasted several weeks futilely searching for a southern passage out of James Bay.

The Trial of Robert Juet

By this time, the crew was openly questioning and doubting their captain. Hudson had passed up an opportunity to load up the ship with fowl and fresh food. They could not understand why he wasted so much time going south. They believed that he should have returned the ship to Hudson Bay and sailed west.

Juet stirred things up, openly complaining about Hudson's aimless wandering. Hudson responded by accusing Juet of being disloyal. After being accused, Juet asked for a trial in front of the ship's crew.

The trial was held on September 10. Juet's shipmates testified that he was responsible for

inciting past problems. Other testimony said that after they left Iceland, Juet "threatened to turne the head of the ship home from the action."[10] Crewmen Philip Staffe and Arnold Lodlo testified against Juet. They said that Juet persuaded them to keep their muskets loaded and their swords ready because the weapons would be needed before the long voyage ended. Their words further implicated Hudson's first mate.

Juet gave his own testimony, but it was very unconvincing. According to crewman Thomas Woodhouse, "After the master had examined and heard with fairness what Juet could say for himself, there proved to be so many great abuses, mutinous matters and action against the master, that there was danger in letting them go on any longer; that it was time to punish and cut off any later occasions of such mutinies."[11]

Juet was removed from his position as first mate and replaced by Robert Bylot. Francis Clement, who had been one of Juet's allies, was replaced as boatswain by William Wilson. Hudson was fair and forgiving. According to Woodhouse, he promised Juet and Clement that if they behaved themselves in the future and for the remainder of the voyage, "he would be a meanes for their good, and that he would forget injuries."[12]

A BITTER WINTER

While Hudson could say that he could forgive past injuries, Juet could not. His resentment festered and he plotted his revenge. He found other crewmen to side with him. Hudson never restored real order amongst his crew.

But even the crewmen who were still loyal to Hudson were losing their faith in him. On one occasion, the *Discovery* was wedged in some rocks for around twelve hours. Crewman Phillip Staffe had warned Hudson of the impending danger, but Hudson ignored him. On another occasion, Hudson lost one of the ship's anchors.

By the end of October, Hudson realized that it was time to quit searching for the elusive passage. Snow covered the ground, and the harsh storms told Hudson it was time to settle in for the winter. By November 10, the *Discovery* and its crew were frozen in for the season.

Hudson could not have picked a more desolate and depressing place to spend a winter with a restless and dispirited crew. Hudson's crew endured frostbite and the swollen limbs, festering wounds, and pulpy gums brought on by scurvy. Prickett made note of their collective misery by writing, "To speake of all our trouble in this time of winter . . . bee too tedious."[13]

The last voyage of Henry Hudson, after his crew mutinied and placed him on a type of boat called a shallop. John Collier painted this scene showing the doomed explorer. With Hudson in this painting is his son.

● CAST ADRIFT

Even after the warmer weather melted the ice, and their voyage resumed, and Hudson continued to make decisions that puzzled and appalled his crew. He removed Bylot as his first mate and replaced him with a man who could not read or write. According to Prickett, the crew believed that Hudson would "take the ship wherever the master pleased."[14]

By then, most of the crew were convinced that Hudson was leading them on an endless journey to nowhere. If their captain would not return their ship to England, they would do it themselves. On or about June 22, 1611, the fourth and final voyage of Henry Hudson abruptly ended with the mutiny led by Wilson and Greene. Instead of searching for a Northwest Passage, Hudson probably spent his final days vainly searching and hoping for a ship to rescue him and the few sickly crewmen who were set adrift with him and his son in the shallop.

● A DEADLY MEETING

Greene assumed command of the other mutineers and took them on the long, arduous, and perilous journey home. Juet and Bylot had a heated argument about the return course. Bylot insisted on a northeasterly course, and Juet argued that they

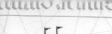

should head northwest. Bylot was correct and fortunately, Greene sided with him. Bylot's route got the *Discovery* back to Digges Island in late July.

When the mutineers set foot on the island they encountered some Inuit who appeared to be friendly. They arranged to meet with the Inuit the next day to trade for some venison. The meeting was an ambush. The Inuit attacked the mutineers, who had to flee for their lives. Greene was killed, and three other mutineers later died from wounds they sustained during the ambush.

A Journey Fueled by Hunger

Following Greene's death, Bylot assumed command of the ship. By that time, only nine of the mutineers were still alive. All of the survivors were sickly and starving. They made two cautious journeys back to Digges Island to replenish their rapidly dwindling supply of food.

They were able to kill around three hundred birds and preserve them in salt. Then they set sail for the southern tip of Greenland. Each crewman was given a daily ration of half a bird to sustain him on the journey.

The meager rations were supplemented by anything that was considered edible. Juet found that by burning away the feathers of the discarded skins, a little extra meat could be salvaged from the birds. In his journal, Prickett noted that garbage was not thrown away. Crewman Bennett Mathues found that, after collecting the bones of the birds, he could "fry them with candle greese till they were crisp, when with vinegar put to them they made a good dish."[15]

No Justice for Hudson

After reaching the southeast coast of Greenland, they set their course to reach Ireland. On September 6, the surviving mutineers sighted the southwestern coast of Ireland. A local fishing boat towed them to shore. The mutineers traded some of the ship's equipment for food, and they gorged themselves. On October 11, 1611, the *Discovery* returned to London.

In November 1611, English maritime officials questioned the mutineers. There were further inquiries, tribunals, and reprimands, but none of the mutineers was ever convicted of a crime. They had destroyed much of Hudson's journal, which contained entries that would have incriminated many of them.

In 1618, Prickett, Edward Wilson, and Frances Clement were formally charged with murdering Hudson and the other crewmen who were cast adrift. An English translation of the Latin version of the original court document charged them with "the ejection of Henry Hudson and others from the ship the 'Discovery' in a boat called a shallop,

without food and drink and other necessaries, and the murder of the same."[16]

All three men pled not guilty. They also claimed that they did not flee after Hudson and the other crewmen were cast adrift. An English translation of the court record documents that they were tried on July 24, 1618.

Unlike another court document, the word murder was not used this time. It merely states that the three men were not guilty of "feloniously pinioning and putting Henry Hudson, master of the 'Discovery' out of the same ship with eight more of his company into a shallop in the Isle in [parts of] America without meat, drink, clothes or other provision, whereby they died."[17]

All three of the accused steadfastly claimed that Greene, William Wilson, and the other deceased mutineers were really the ones to blame. That was an easy and convenient defense, since the dead could not defend themselves. The accused also made a credible claim that they were in danger of starving to death. They also pointed out that no one was wounded or injured before Hudson and the others were cast adrift.

After deliberating for an unrecorded amount of time, a fourteen-man jury found the trio not guilty. It is not too surprising that they were acquitted. During the seven years between their return to England and their trial, the rivalry between England

and Holland for commercial advantages had intensified. The potential for economic advantage was greater than the need for justice.

Prickett went on to make several voyages for London companies. Although he was never charged with being a mutineer, Bylot, the navigator on the *Discovery*, did the same.

The Importance and Lasting Influence of Henry Hudson

While some would call Hudson a failure for never finding a Northeast or Northwest Passage, he can hardly be faulted for failing to find something that never existed. Hudson may have even harbored some secret doubts about whether such a passage existed. During his fourth and final voyage, he told Bylot, "If the passage be found, I confess that there is something gained in the distance, but nothing in the navigation. For allow if this passage falls into the South Sea; if it does, little good is like to ensue because of the hazard of cold, of ice, and of unknown seas which experience must teach us."[18] His failure to find such a passage helped to end the firmly held belief that a navigable waterway around or through North America would lead to Asia. Today Hudson is immortalized by a river, a bay, and a strait that are named for him.

His first voyage enabled the British to enter the lucrative whaling trade. His third voyage and

Henry Hudson was the first European to explore so far up the Hudson River. This is why the river bears his name today.

explorations allowed the Dutch to colonize North America in New York, Connecticut, and Delaware. Although the English seized New Amsterdam in 1664, the Dutch remained an influential presence in several eastern states, especially New York state. The four decades that the Dutch ruled New Amsterdam established legal norms, including women owning property in their own name. Place names also came from the Dutch, including Brooklyn, the Bronx, and Staten Island. The Dutch also contributed social customs, including a religion not easily overturned by the British.

The Dutch were among the most liberal thinkers of their age, and the small enclave they founded on the tip of a slender island promoted religious tolerance, ethnic diversity, and the idea that merit supersedes class distinction. This enclave was founded on commerce and not religious ideology. It welcomed all who could make it prosper regardless of race, religion, or national origins. This enclave, Manhattan Island, grew to a global center of commerce and the melting pot of the United States.

This is Henry Hudson's lasting legacy and the United States is much richer for it. Unfortunately, the colonization of the continent by European nations also contributed to the destruction of the Mohawk, Mohican, and several other Indian tribes.

Hudson's explorations of the Arctic Ocean northwest of Canada helped the British to establish the Hudson's Bay Company, which monopolized fur trading in that area. The company was founded in 1670 after the British drove out the Dutch.

While traveling under the most difficult conditions—unrelenting fog, bitter cold, swirling snow, gripping ice, and perilous icebergs and ice floes—Hudson explored and charted unknown territory. His pioneering explorations made things much easier for the explorers who followed him.

If Hudson had a fatal flaw, it was his obsession with finding a passage that was not there. His obsession kept him from controlling a crew that finally turned against him.

Chapter Notes

Chapter 1. Mutiny!

1. Llewelyn Powys, *Henry Hudson* (New York: Harper & Brother Publishers, 1928), p. 147.

2. Ibid., p. 152.

3. Donald S. Johnson, *Charting the Sea of Darkness: The Four Voyages of Henry Hudson* (New York: Kodansha International, 1993), p. 170.

4. M. B. Synge, *A Book of Discovery* (Chapel Hill, N.C.: Yesterday's Classics, 2007), p. 271.

5. Richard Woodman, *A Brief History of Mutiny* (New York: Carroll & Graf Publishers, 2005), p. 39.

6. Lawrence Millman, "Looking for Henry Hudson," *Smithsonian*, October 1999.

7. Powys, p. 160.

8. Johnson, p. 179.

Chapter 3. Whales, Fog, and Icebergs

1. Fergus Fleming, *Off the Map: Tales of Endurance and Exploration* (New York: Atlantic Monthly Press, 2006), p. 87.

2. Donald S. Johnson, *Charting the Sea of Darkness: The Four Voyages of Henry Hudson* (New York: Kodansha International, 1993), p. 26.

3. Ibid., p. 41.

4. Ibid., p. 43.

Chapter 4. An Unhappy Crew

1. Llewelyn Powys, *Henry Hudson* (New York: Harper & Brothers Publishers, 1928), p. 45.

2. Donald S. Johnson, *Charting the Sea of Darkness: The Four Voyages of Henry Hudson* (New York: Kodansha International, 1993), p. 56.

3. Ibid., pp. 58–59.

4. Edgar Mayhew Bacon, *Henry Hudson: His Times and Voyages* (New York: G.P. Putnam's Sons, 1907), p. 73.

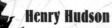
5. Samuel Purchas, *Henry Hudson's Voyages from Purchas His Pilgrimes* (Ann Arbor, Mich.: University Microfilms, Inc.), p. 578.

6. Ibid., p. 578.

7. Bacon, p. 80.

8. Purchas, p. 579.

9. Powys, p. 58.

Chapter 5. Fighting to Sail Again

1. Donald S. Johnson, *Charting the Sea of Darkness: The Four Voyages of Henry Hudson* (New York: Kodansha International, 1993), p. 86.

2. Ibid., p. 87.

3. Ibid., p. 86.

Chapter 6. A Trip to America

1. Samuel Purchas, *Henry Hudson's Voyages from Purchas His Pilgrimes* (Ann Arbor, Mich.: University Microfilms, Inc.), p. 581.

2. Edgar Mayhew Bacon, *Henry Hudson: His Times and Voyages* (New York: G.P. Putnam's Sons, 1907), p. 117.

3. Llewelyn Powys, *Henry Hudson* (New York: Harper & Brother Publishers, 1928), p. 92.

4. Purchas, p. 592.

5. Donald S. Johnson, *Charting the Sea of Darkness: The Four Voyages of Henry Hudson* (New York: Kodansha International, 1993), p. 116.

6. Bacon, p. 131.

7. Johnson, p. 116.

8. Samuel Purchas, *Hakluytus Posthumus: Or Purchas His Pilgrimes* (Glasgow, Scotland: James MacLehose and Sons, 1906), p. 364.

9. Johnson, p. 117.

10. Ibid., p. 118.

11. New York Historical Society, *Collections of New York Historical Society for the Year* (New York: I. Riley, 1841), p. 325.

12. Johnson, p. 121.

13. Bacon, p. 170–171.

Chapter 7. The Last Voyage

1. Llewelyn Powys, *Henry Hudson* (New York: Harper & Brother Publishers, 1928), p. 58.

2. Ibid., p. 72.

3. Ibid., p. 73.

4. Ibid., pp. 125–126.

5. Brendan Lehane, *The Northwest Passage* (Alexandria, Va.: Time-Life Books, 1981), p. 48.

6. Powys, p. 129.

7. Donald S. Johnson, *Charting the Sea of Darkness: The Four Voyages of Henry Hudson* (New York: Kodansha International, 1993), p. 160.

8. John Barrow, *A Chronological History of Voyages Into the Arctic Regions* (London: John Murray, 1818), p. 189.

9. Johnson, p. 160.

10. Powys, p. 142.

11. Johnson, pp. 189–190.

12. Powys, p. 143.

13. Lawrence Millman, "Looking for Henry Hudson," *Smithsonian*, October 1999.

14. Johnson, p. 176.

15. Powys, p. 181.

16. Ibid., p. 196.

17. Ibid., p. 193.

18. Edward Struzik, *Northwest Passage: The Quest for an Arctic Route to the East* (Toronto: Key Porter Books, 1991), p. 45.

Glossary

adroit—Cleverly skillful.

boatswain—A ship's officer in charge of the hull and all the related equipment.

bulrush—An aquatic plant also known as a cattail.

cartographer—A mapmaker.

coerced—Compelled to act because of force or threats.

crow's nest—A platform high on the mast of a sailing ship that is used as a lookout post.

floes—Large flat sheets of floating ice.

hallucinate—To see something that is not there.

headland—High land that juts out into a body of water.

hold—The area of a ship where the cargo is stored.

insubordinate—Unwilling to submit to authority.

marooned—Being left in isolation with no hope of escape.

mutiny—The revolt of a ship's crew against the captain or some other superior officer.

persecute—To harass or oppress continuously.

propensity—A natural tendency.

scurvy—A disease caused by a lack of vitamin C.

shallop—A small, open boat powered by oars or sails.

sound—A large, broad inlet of the ocean.

strait—A passageway connecting two bodies of water.

stymied—Unable to move because of an obstacle or obstacles.

subarctic—Regions immediately outside of the Arctic Circle.

venison—Deer meat.

Further Reading

BOOKS

Blue, Rose, and Corinne J. Naden. *Exploring Northeastern America*. Chicago: Raintree, 2003.

Doak, Robin S. *Hudson: Henry Hudson Searches for a Passage to Asia*. Minneapolis, Minn.: Compass Point Books, 2003.

Gleason, Carrie. *Henry Hudson: Seeking the Northwest Passage*. New York: Crabtree, 2005.

Kimmel, Elizabeth Cody. *The Look-It-Up Book of Explorers*. New York: Random House, 2004.

Otfinoski, Steven. *Henry Hudson: In Search of the Northwest Passage*. New York: Marshall Cavendish Benchmark, 2007.

Saffer, Barbara. *Henry Hudson: Ill-Fated Explorer of North America's Coast*. Philadelphia: Chelsea House, 2002.

Shorto, Russell. *The Island at the Center of the World*. New York: Random House, Vintage Index, 2004.

INTERNET ADDRESSES

Big Apple History: Early New York—Henry Hudson
<http://pbskids.org/bigapplehistory/early/topic1.html>

Henry Hudson, Half Moon, and Exploration of the Hudson River
<http://www.hrmm.org/halfmoon/halfmoon.htm>

The Life and Voyages of Henry Hudson, English Explorer and Navigator
<http://www.ianchadwick.com/hudson/>

Index

110